I AM
SOMEBODY!

AMERICAN BIBLE SOCIETY
NEW YORK

I Am Somebody!

Good News Translation

This is a Portion of Holy Scripture in the *Good News Translation*. The American Bible Society is a not-for-profit organization which publishes the Scriptures without doctrinal note or comment. Since 1816, its single mission has been to make the Bible easily available to every person in a language and format each can understand and afford. Working toward this goal, the ABS is a member of the United Bible Societies, a worldwide effort that extends to more than 200 countries and territories. You are urged to read the Bible and to share it with others. For a free catalog of other Scripture publications, call the American Bible Society at 1-800-32-BIBLE, or write to 1865 Broadway, New York, NY 10023-7505. Visit the ABS website! **www.americanbible.org**

Copyright © American Bible Society, 1992

ISBN 1-58516-365-1

Printed in the United States of America
Eng. Port. GNT560P – 104718
ABS – 6/02 – 2,500 – 33,500 – CG13

INTRODUCTION

I'm somebody!
  Somebody created to be like God.
  Somebody for whom Christ gave his life!
  Yes, I'm somebody—
    with special gifts for service
    with something to share
    with decisions to make
    with someone at my side.
  In all the ways that I'm somebody, you're somebody too! So read the Scripture passages in this book and consider what makes each of us somebody and what it means to be somebody. You'll discover that the same things that make us somebody also make us somebody special.

CONTENTS

I'm Somebody Created To Be
  Like God...............................1

I'm Somebody Because Christ Gave
  Himself For Me........................7

I'm Somebody With Special Gifts For
  Service..............................13

I'm Somebody With Something
  To Share 21

I'm Somebody With Decisions
  To Make 31

I'm Somebody With Someone At
  My Side..............................39

I'M SOMEBODY CREATED TO BE LIKE GOD

All were created to share in the likeness of God, which the Bible often describes as "the Glory of God"

We are created to be like God

Then God said, "And now we will make human beings; they will be like us and resemble us. They will have power over the fish, the birds, and all animals, domestic and wild, large and small." So God created human beings, making them to be like himself. He created them male and female, blessed them, and said, "Have many children, so that your descendants will live all over the earth and bring it under their control. I am putting you in charge of the fish, the birds, and all the wild animals. I have provided all kinds of grain and all kinds of fruit for you to eat; but for all the wild animals and for all the birds I have provided grass and leafy plants for food"—and it was done. God looked at everything he had made, and he was very pleased. Evening passed and morning came—that was the sixth day.

Genesis 1.26-31

We are crowned with glory and honor

O LORD, our Lord,
>   your greatness is seen in all
>   the world!
Your praise reaches up to the
>   heavens;
>   it is sung by children and
>   babies.
You are safe and secure from all
>   your enemies;
>   you stop anyone who opposes
>   you.

When I look at the sky, which
>   you have made,
>   at the moon and the stars,
>   which you set in their
>   places—
what are human beings, that
>   you think of them;
>   mere mortals, that you care for
>   them?

Yet you made them inferior only
>   to yourself;
>   you crowned them with glory
>   and honor.
You appointed them rulers over
>   everything you made;
>   you placed them over all
>   creation:

> sheep and cattle, and the wild animals too;
> the birds and the fish
> and the creatures in the seas.

O Lord, our Lord,
> your greatness is seen in all the world!

Psalm 8

God's glory is seen in Christian living

Dear friends, let us love one another, because love comes from God. Whoever loves is a child of God and knows God. Whoever does not love does not know God, for God is love. And God showed his love for us by sending his only Son into the world, so that we might have life through him. This is what love is: it is not that we have loved God, but that he loved us and sent his Son to be the means by which our sins are forgiven.

Dear friends, if this is how God loved us, then we should love one another. No one has ever seen God, but if we love one another, God lives in union with us, and his love is made perfect in us.

We are sure that we live in union with God and that he lives in union with us, because he has given us his Spirit. And we have seen and tell others that the Father sent his Son to be the Savior of the world. If we declare that Jesus is the Son of God, we live in union with God and God lives in union with us. And we ourselves know and believe the love which God has for us.

God is love, and those who live in love live in union with God and God lives in union with them. Love is made perfect in us in order that we may have courage on the Judgment Day; and we will have it because our life in this world is the same as Christ's. There is no fear in love; perfect love drives out all fear. So then, love has not been made perfect in anyone who is afraid, because fear has to do with punishment.

We love because God first loved us. If we say we love God, but hate others, we are liars. For we cannot love God, whom we have not seen, if we do not love others, whom we have seen. The command that Christ has given us is this: whoever loves God must love others also.

1 John 4.7-21

Our bodies are for God's glory

Someone will say, "I am allowed to do anything." Yes; but not everything is good for you. I could say that I am allowed to do anything, but I am not going to let anything make me its slave. Someone else will say, "Food is for the stomach, and the stomach is for food." Yes; but God will put an end to both. The body is not to be used for sexual immorality, but to serve the Lord; and the Lord provides for the body. God raised the Lord from death, and he will also raise us by his power.

You know that your bodies are parts of the body of Christ. Shall I take a part of Christ's body and make it part of the body of a prostitute? Impossible! Or perhaps you don't know that the man who joins his body to a prostitute becomes physically one with her? The scripture says quite plainly, "The two will become one body." But he who joins himself to the Lord becomes spiritually one with him.

Avoid immorality. Any other sin a man commits does not affect his body; but the man who is guilty of sexual immorality sins against his own body. Don't you know that your body is the temple of the Holy Spirit, who lives in you and who was given to you by God? You do not belong to yourselves but to God; he bought you for a price. So use your bodies for God's glory.

1 Corinthians 6.12-20

I'M SOMEBODY BECAUSE CHRIST GAVE HIMSELF FOR ME

This is a central theme of the entire New Testament, and it receives major emphasis in the book of Hebrews.

Christ became a human like me

Since the children, as he calls them, are people of flesh and blood, Jesus himself became like them and shared their human nature. He did this so that through his death he might destroy the Devil, who has the power over death, and in this way set free those who were slaves all their lives because of their fear of death. For it is clear that it is not the angels that he helps. Instead, he helps the descendants of Abraham. This means that he had to become like his people in every way, in order to be their faithful and merciful High Priest in his service to God, so that the people's sins would be forgiven. And now he can help those who are tempted, because he himself was tempted and suffered.

Hebrews 2.14-18

He leads me to God

Let us, then, hold firmly to the faith we profess. For we have a great High Priest who has gone into the very presence of God—Jesus, the Son of God. Our High Priest is not one who cannot feel sympathy for our weaknesses. On the contrary, we have a High Priest who was tempted in every way that we are, but did not sin. Let us have confidence, then, and approach God's throne, where there is grace. There we will receive mercy and find grace to help us just when we need it.

Hebrews 4.14-16

In his life on earth Jesus made his prayers and requests with loud cries and tears to God, who could save him from death. Because he was humble and devoted, God heard him. But even though he was God's Son, he learned through his sufferings to be obedient. When he was made perfect, he became the source of eternal salvation for all those who obey him.

Hebrews 5.7-9

He forgives my sins

Every Jewish priest performs his services every day and offers the same sacrifices many times; but these sacrifices can never take away sins. Christ, however, offered one sacrifice for sins, an offering that is effective forever, and then he sat down at the right side of God. There he now waits until God puts his enemies as a footstool under his feet. With one sacrifice, then, he has made perfect forever those who are purified from sin.

And the Holy Spirit also gives us his witness. First he says,
> "This is the covenant that I
> will make with them
> in the days to come, says
> the Lord:
> I will put my laws in their
> hearts
> and write them on their
> minds."

And then he says, "I will not remember their sins and evil deeds any longer." So when these have been forgiven, an offering to take away sins is no longer needed.

Hebrews 10.11-18

He gives me endurance

As for us, we have this large crowd of witnesses around us. So then, let us rid ourselves of everything that gets in the way, and of the sin which holds on to us so tightly, and let us run with determination the race that lies before us. Let us keep our eyes fixed on Jesus, on whom our faith depends from beginning to end. He did not give up because of the cross! On the contrary, because of the joy that was waiting for him, he thought nothing of the disgrace of dying on the cross, and he is now seated at the right side of God's throne.

Hebrews 12.1,2

He gives me inner strength

Keep on loving one another as Christians. Remember to welcome strangers in your homes. There were some who did that and welcomed angels without knowing it. Remember those who are in prison, as though you were in prison with them. Remember those who are suffering, as though you were suffering as they are.

Marriage is to be honored by all, and husbands and wives must be faithful to each other. God will judge those who are immoral and those who commit adultery.

Keep your lives free from the love of money, and be satisfied with what you have. For God has said, "I will never leave you; I will never abandon you." Let us be bold, then, and say,

>"The Lord is my helper,
>   I will not be afraid.
>   What can anyone do to me?"

Remember your former leaders, who spoke God's message to you. Think back on how they lived and died, and imitate their faith. Jesus Christ is the same yesterday, today, and forever. Do not let all kinds of strange teachings lead you from the right way. It is good to receive inner strength from God's grace, and not by obeying rules about foods; those who obey these rules have not been helped by them.

Hebrews 13.1-9

I'M SOMEBODY WITH SPECIAL GIFTS FOR SERVICE

All of us possess unique gifts, but there are also many special gifts that we have that equip us for the service of others.

The gift of encouragement

Brother Philemon, every time I pray, I mention you and give thanks to my God. For I hear of your love for all of God's people and the faith you have in the Lord Jesus. My prayer is that our fellowship with you as believers will bring about a deeper understanding of every blessing which we have in our life in union with Christ. Your love, dear brother, has brought me great joy and much encouragement! You have cheered the hearts of all of God's people.

Philemon 4-7

The gift of discipline

All this I do for the gospel's sake, in order to share in its blessings. Surely you know that many runners take part in a race, but only one of them wins the prize. Run, then, in such a way as to win the prize. Every athlete in training submits to strict discipline, in order to be crowned with a wreath that will not last; but we do it for one that will last forever. That is why I run straight for the finish line; that is why I am like a boxer who does not waste his punches. I harden my body with blows and bring it under complete control, to keep myself from being disqualified after having called others to the contest.

1 Corinthians 9.23-27

The gift of accepting others

Welcome those who are weak in faith, but do not argue with them about their personal opinions. Some people's faith allows them to eat anything, but the person who is weak in the faith eats only vegetables. The person who will eat anything is not to despise the one who doesn't; while the one who eats only vegetables is not to pass judgment on the one who will eat anything; for God has accepted that person. Who are you to judge the servants of someone else? It is their own Master who will decide whether they succeed or fail. And they will succeed, because the Lord is able to make them succeed.

Some people think that a certain day is more important than other days, while others think that all days are the same. We each should firmly make up our own minds. Those who think highly of a certain day do so in honor of the Lord; those who will eat anything do so in honor of the Lord, because they give thanks to God for the food. Those who refuse to eat certain things do so in honor of the Lord, and they give thanks to God. We do not live for ourselves only, and we do not die for ourselves only. If we live, it is for the Lord that we live, and if we die, it is for the Lord that we die. So whether we live or die, we belong to the Lord. For Christ died and rose to life in order to be the Lord of the living and of the dead. You then, who eat only vegetables—why do you pass judgment on others? And you who eat anything—why do you despise other believers? All of us will stand before God to be judged by him. For the scripture says,

> "As surely as I am the living
> God, says the Lord,
> everyone will kneel before
> me,
> and everyone will confess
> that I am God."

Every one of us, then, will have to give an account to God.

Romans 14.1-12

The gift of forgiving

Now, if anyone has made somebody sad, he has not done it to me but to all of you—in part, at least. (I say this because I do not want to be too hard on him.) It is enough that this person has been punished in this way by most of you. Now, however, you should forgive him and encourage him, in order to keep him from becoming so sad as to give up completely. And so I beg you to let him know that you really do love him. I wrote you that letter because I wanted to find out how well you had stood the test and whether you are always ready to obey my instructions. When you forgive people for what they have done, I forgive them too. For when I forgive—if, indeed, I need to forgive anything—I do it in Christ's presence because of you, in order to keep Satan from getting the upper hand over us; for we know what his plans are.

2 Corinthians 2.5-11

The gift of love

Be under obligation to no one—the only obligation you have is to love one another. Whoever does this has obeyed the Law. The commandments, "Do not commit adultery; do not commit murder; do not steal; do not desire what belongs to someone else"—all these, and any others besides, are summed up in the one command, "Love your neighbor as you love yourself." If you love others, you will never do them wrong; to love, then, is to obey the whole Law.

Romans 13.8-10

The gift of prayer

I thank my God for you every time I think of you; and every time I pray for you all, I pray with joy because of the way in which you have helped me in the work of the gospel from the very first day until now. And so I am sure that God, who began this good work in you, will carry it on until it is finished on the Day of Christ Jesus. You are always in my heart! And so it is only right for me to feel as I do about you. For you have all shared with me in this privilege that God has given me, both now that I am in prison and also while I was free to defend the gospel and establish it firmly. God is my witness that I tell the truth when I say that my deep feeling for you all comes from the heart of Christ Jesus himself.

I pray that your love will keep on growing more and more, together with true knowledge and perfect judgment, so that you will be able to choose what is best. Then you will be free from all impurity and blame on the Day of Christ. Your lives will be filled with the truly good qualities which only Jesus Christ can produce, for the glory and praise of God.

Philippians 1.3-11

The gift of thankfulness

Let us give thanks to the God and Father of our Lord Jesus Christ, the merciful Father, the God from whom all help comes! He helps us in all our troubles, so that we are able to help others who have all kinds of troubles, using the same help that we ourselves have received from God. Just as we have a share in Christ's many sufferings, so also through Christ we share in God's great help. If we suffer, it is for your help and salvation; if we are helped, then you too are helped and given the strength to endure with patience the same sufferings that we also endure. So our hope in you is never shaken; we know that just as you share in our sufferings, you also share in the help we receive.

2 Corinthians 1.3-7

The source of all gifts

There are different kinds of spiritual gifts, but the same Spirit gives them. There are different ways of serving, but the same Lord is served. There are different abilities to perform service, but the same God gives ability to all for their particular service. The Spirit's presence is shown in some way in each person for the good of all. The Spirit gives one person a message full of wisdom, while to another person the same Spirit gives a message full of knowledge. One and the same Spirit gives faith to one person, while to another person he gives the power to heal. The Spirit gives one person the power to work miracles; to another, the gift of speaking God's message; and to yet another, the ability to tell the difference between gifts that come from the Spirit and those that do not. To one person he gives the ability to speak in strange tongues, and to another he gives the ability to explain what is said. But it is one and the same Spirit who does all this; as he wishes, he gives a different gift to each person.

1 Corinthians 12.4-11

I'M SOMEBODY WITH SOMETHING TO SHARE

If we ask ourselves what we have that can be shared with others, the answer is our Lord and ourselves.

I can share my Lord with relatives

The next day John was standing there again with two of his disciples, when he saw Jesus walking by. "There is the Lamb of God!" he said.

The two disciples heard him say this and went with Jesus. Jesus turned, saw them following him, and asked, "What are you looking for?"

They answered, "Where do you live, Rabbi?" (This word means "Teacher.")

"Come and see," he answered. (It was then about four o'clock in the afternoon.) So they went with him and saw where he lived, and spent the rest of that day with him.

One of them was Andrew, Simon Peter's brother. At once he found his brother Simon and told him, "We have found the Messiah." (This word means "Christ.") Then he took Simon to Jesus.

Jesus looked at him and said, "Your name is Simon son of John, but you will be called Cephas." (This is the same as Peter and means "a rock.")

John 1.35-42

I can share my Lord with friends

The next day Jesus decided to go to Galilee. He found Philip and said to him, "Come with me!" (Philip was from Bethsaida, the town where Andrew and Peter lived.) Philip found Nathanael and told him, "We have found the one whom Moses wrote about in the book of the Law and whom the prophets also wrote about. He is Jesus son of Joseph, from Nazareth."

John 1.43-45

I can share my Lord with strangers

While Paul was waiting in Athens for Silas and Timothy, he was greatly upset when he noticed how full of idols the city was. So he held discussions in the synagogue with the Jews and with the Gentiles who worshiped God, and also in the public square every day with the people who happened to come by.

Certain Epicurean and Stoic teachers also debated with him. Some of them asked, "What is this ignorant show-off trying to say?"

Others answered, "He seems to be talking about foreign gods." They said this because Paul was preaching about Jesus and the resurrection. So they took Paul, brought him before the city council, the Areopagus, and said, "We would like to know what this new teaching is that you are talking about. Some of the things we hear you say sound strange to us, and we would like to know what they mean." (For all the citizens of Athens and the foreigners who lived there liked to spend all their time telling and hearing the latest new thing.)

Paul stood up in front of the city council and said, "I see that in every way you Athenians are very religious. For as I walked through your city and looked at the places where you worship, I found an altar on which is written, 'To an Unknown God.' That which you worship, then, even though you do not know it, is what I now proclaim to you. God, who made the world and everything in it, is Lord of heaven and earth and does not live in temples made by human hands. Nor does he need anything that we can supply by working for him, since it is he himself who gives life and breath and everything else to everyone. From one human being he created all races of people and made them live throughout the whole earth. He himself fixed beforehand the exact times and the limits of the places where they would live. He did this so that they would look for him, and perhaps find him as they felt around for him. Yet God is actually not far from any one of us; as someone has said,

> 'In him we live and move and
> exist.'

It is as some of your poets have said,

> 'We too are his children.'

Since we are God's children, we should not suppose that his nature is anything like an image of gold or silver or stone, shaped by the human art and skill. God has overlooked the times when people did not know him, but now he commands all of them everywhere to turn away from their evil ways. For he has fixed a day in which he will judge the whole world with justice by means of a man he has chosen. He has given proof of this to everyone by raising that man from death!"

When they heard Paul speak about a raising from death, some of them made fun of him, but others said, "We want to hear you speak about this again." And so Paul left the meeting. Some men joined him and believed, among whom was Dionysius, a member of the council; there was also a woman named Damaris, and some other people.

Acts 17.16-34

I can share myself through humble service

It was now the day before the Passover Festival. Jesus knew that the hour had come for him to leave this world and go to the Father. He had always loved those in the world who were his own, and he loved them to the very end.

Jesus and his disciples were at supper. The Devil had already put into the heart of Judas, the son of Simon Iscariot, the thought of betraying Jesus. Jesus knew that the Father had given him complete power; he knew that he had come from God and was going to God. So he rose from the table, took off his outer garment, and tied a towel around his waist. Then he poured some water into a washbasin and began to wash the disciples' feet and dry them with the towel around his waist. He came to Simon Peter, who said to him, "Are you going to wash my feet, Lord?"

Jesus answered him, "You do not understand now what I am doing, but you will understand later."

Peter declared, "Never at any time will you wash my feet!"

"If I do not wash your feet," Jesus answered, "you will no longer be my disciple."

Simon Peter answered, "Lord, do not wash only my feet, then! Wash my hands and head, too!"

Jesus said, "Those who have taken a bath are completely clean and do not have to wash themselves, except for their feet. All of you are clean—all except one." (Jesus already knew who was going to betray him; that is why he said, "All of you, except one, are clean.")

After Jesus had washed their feet, he put his outer garment back on and returned to his place at the table. "Do you understand what I have just done to you?" he asked. "You call me Teacher and Lord, and it is right that you do so, because that is what I am. I, your Lord and Teacher, have just washed your feet. You, then, should wash one another's feet. I have set an example for you, so that you will do just what I have done for you. I am telling you the truth: no slaves are greater than their master, and no messengers are greater than the one who sent them. Now that you know this truth, how happy you will be if you put it into practice!"

John 13.1-17

I can share myself through unselfish love

Jesus said, "Now the Son of Man's glory is revealed; now God's glory is revealed through him. And if God's glory is revealed through him, then God will reveal the glory of the Son of Man in himself, and he will do so at once. My children, I shall not be with you very much longer. You will look for me; but I tell you now what I told the Jewish authorities, 'You cannot go where I am going.' And now I give you a new commandment: love one another. As I have loved you, so you must love one another. If you have love for one another, then everyone will know that you are my disciples."

John 13.31-35

I can share myself through giving whatever I have

After this, Jesus went across Lake Galilee (or, Lake Tiberias, as it is also called). A large crowd followed him, because they had seen his miracles of healing the sick. Jesus went up a hill and sat down with his disciples. The time for the Passover Festival was near. Jesus looked around and saw that a large crowd was coming to him, so he asked Philip, "Where can we buy enough food to feed all these people?" (He said this to test Philip; actually he already knew what he would do.)

Philip answered, "For everyone to have even a little, it would take more than two hundred silver coins to buy enough bread."

Another one of his disciples, Andrew, who was Simon Peter's brother, said, "There is a boy here who has five loaves of barley bread and two fish. But they will certainly not be enough for all these people."

"Make the people sit down," Jesus told them. (There was a lot of grass there.) So all the people sat down; there were about five thousand men. Jesus took the bread, gave thanks to God, and distributed it to the people who were sitting there. He did the same with the fish, and they all had as much as they wanted. When they were all full, he said to his disciples, "Gather the pieces left over; let us not waste a bit." So they gathered them all and filled twelve baskets with the pieces left over from the five barley loaves which the people had eaten.

Seeing this miracle that Jesus had performed, the people there said, "Surely this is the Prophet who was to come into the world!" Jesus knew that they were about to come and seize him in order to make him king by force; so he went off again to the hills by himself.

John 6.1-15

I'M SOMEBODY WITH DECISIONS TO MAKE

The decisions that we make help determine the kind of people we are.

Decisions determine my destiny

Jesus said:

"When the Son of Man comes as King and all the angels with him, he will sit on his royal throne, and the people of all the nations will be gathered before him. Then he will divide them into two groups, just as a shepherd separates the sheep from the goats. He will put the righteous people at his right and the others at his left. Then the King will say to the people on his right, 'Come, you that are blessed by my Father! Come and possess the kingdom which has been prepared for you ever since the creation of the world. I was hungry and you fed me, thirsty and you gave me a drink; I was a stranger and you received me in your homes, naked and you clothed me; I was sick and you took care of me, in prison and you visited me.' The righteous will then answer him, 'When, Lord, did we ever see you hungry and feed you, or thirsty and give you a drink? When did we ever see you a stranger and welcome you in our homes, or naked and clothe you? When did we ever see you sick or in prison, and visit you?' The King will reply, 'I tell you, whenever you did this for one of the least important of these followers of mine, you did it for me!'

"Then he will say to those on his left, 'Away from me, you that are under God's curse! Away to the eternal fire which has been prepared for the Devil and his angels! I was hungry but you would not feed me, thirsty but you would not give me a drink; I was a stranger but you would not welcome me in your homes, naked but you would not clothe me; I was sick and in prison but you would not take care of me.' Then they will answer him, 'When, Lord, did we ever see you hungry or thirsty or a stranger or naked or sick or in prison, and we would not help you?' The King will reply, 'I tell you, whenever you refused to help one of these least important ones, you refused to help me.' These, then, will be sent off to eternal punishment, but the righteous will go to eternal life."

Matthew 25.31-46

My decisions affect others

Now the snake was the most cunning animal that the LORD God had made. The snake asked the woman, "Did God really tell you not to eat fruit from any tree in the garden?"

"We may eat the fruit of any tree in the garden," the woman answered, "except the tree in the middle of it. God told us not to eat the fruit of that tree or even touch it; if we do, we will die."

The snake replied, "That's not true; you will not die. God said that because he knows that when you eat it, you will be like God and know what is good and what is bad."

The woman saw how beautiful the tree was and how good its fruit would be to eat, and she thought how wonderful it would be to become wise. So she took some of the fruit and ate it. Then she gave some to her husband, and he also ate it. As soon as they had eaten it, they were given understanding and realized that they were naked; so they sewed fig leaves together and covered themselves.

That evening they heard the Lord God walking in the garden, and they hid from him among the trees. But the Lord God called out to the man, "Where are you?"

He answered, "I heard you in the garden; I was afraid and hid from you, because I was naked."

"Who told you that you were naked?" God asked. "Did you eat the fruit that I told you not to eat?"

The man answered, "The woman you put here with me gave me the fruit, and I ate it."

The Lord God asked the woman, "Why did you do this?"

She replied, "The snake tricked me into eating it."

Then the LORD God said to the snake, "You will be punished for this; you alone of all the animals must bear this curse: From now on you will crawl on your belly, and you will have to eat dust as long as you live. I will make you and the woman hate each other; her offspring and yours will always be enemies. Her offspring will crush your head, and you will bite her offspring's heel."

And he said to the woman, "I will increase your trouble in pregnancy and your pain in giving birth. In spite of this, you will still have desire for your husband, yet you will be subject to him."

And he said to the man, "You listened to your wife and ate the fruit which I told you not to eat. Because of what you have done, the ground will be under a curse. You will have to work hard all your life to make it produce enough food for you. It will produce weeds and thorns, and you will have to eat wild plants. You will have to work hard and sweat to make the soil produce anything, until you go back to the soil from which you were formed. You were made from soil, and you will become soil again."

Adam named his wife Eve, because she was the mother of all human beings. And the LORD God made clothes out of animal skins for Adam and his wife, and he clothed them.

Then the LORD God said, "Now these human beings have become like one of us and have knowledge of what is good and what is bad. They must not be allowed to take fruit from the tree that gives life, eat it, and live forever." So the LORD God sent them out of the Garden of Eden and made them cultivate the soil from which they had been formed. Then at the east side of the garden he put living creatures and a flaming sword which turned in all directions. This was to keep anyone from coming near the tree that gives life.

Genesis 3.1-24

Some decisions are difficult to make

Paul wrote:

I want you to know, my friends, that the things that have happened to me have really helped the progress of the gospel. As a result, the whole palace guard and all the others here know that I am in prison because I am a servant of Christ. And my being in prison has given most of the believers more confidence in the Lord, so that they grow bolder all the time to preach the message fearlessly.

Of course some of them preach Christ because they are jealous and quarrelsome, but others from genuine good will. These do so from love, because they know that God has given me the work of defending the gospel. The others do not proclaim Christ sincerely, but from a spirit of selfish ambition; they think that they will make more trouble for me while I am in prison.

It does not matter! I am happy about it—just so Christ is preached in every way possible, whether from wrong or right motives. And I will continue to be happy, because I know that by means of your prayers and the help which comes from the Spirit of Jesus Christ I shall be set free. My deep desire and hope is that I shall never fail in my duty, but that at all times, and especially right now, I shall be full of courage, so that with my whole being I shall bring honor to Christ, whether I live or die. For what is life? To me, it is Christ. Death, then, will bring more. But if by continuing to live I can do more worthwhile work, then I am not sure which I should choose. I am pulled in two directions. I want very much to leave this life and be with Christ, which is a far better thing; but for your sake it is much more important that I remain alive. I am sure of this, and so I know that I will stay. I will stay on with you all, to add to your progress and joy in the faith, so that when I am with you again, you will have even more reason to be proud of me in your life in union with Christ Jesus.

Philippians 1.12-26

Christ will guide my decisions

You are the people of God; he loved you and chose you for his own. So then, you must clothe yourselves with compassion, kindness, humility, gentleness, and patience. Be tolerant with one another and forgive one another whenever any of you has a complaint against someone else. You must forgive one another just as the Lord has forgiven you. And to all these qualities add love, which binds all things together in perfect unity. The peace that Christ gives is to guide you in the decisions you make; for it is to this peace that God has called you together in the one body. And be thankful. Christ's message in all its richness must live in your hearts. Teach and instruct one another with all wisdom. Sing psalms, hymns, and sacred songs; sing to God with thanksgiving in your hearts. Everything you do or say, then, should be done in the name of the Lord Jesus, as you give thanks through him to God the Father.

Colossians 3.12-17

I'M SOMEBODY WITH SOMEONE AT MY SIDE

One of the joys of being a believer is knowing that God's Spirit is always with us.

God's Spirit directs and controls my life

What I say is this: let the Spirit direct your lives, and you will not satisfy the desires of the human nature. For what our human nature wants is opposed to what the Spirit wants, and what the Spirit wants is opposed to what our human nature wants. These two are enemies, and this means that you cannot do what you want to do. If the Spirit leads you, then you are not subject to the Law.

What human nature does is quite plain. It shows itself in immoral, filthy, and indecent actions; in worship of idols and witchcraft. People become enemies and they fight; they become jealous, angry, and ambitious. They separate into parties and groups; they are envious, get drunk, have orgies, and do other things like these. I warn you now as I have before: those who do these things will not possess the Kingdom of God.

But the Spirit produces love, joy, peace, patience, kindness, goodness, faithfulness, humility, and self-control. There is no law against such things as these. And those who belong to Christ Jesus have put to death their human nature with all its passions and desires. The Spirit has given us life; he must also control our lives. We must not be proud or irritate one another or be jealous of one another.

Galatians 5.16-26

God's Spirit teaches me everything

Jesus said:

"If you love me, you will obey my commandments. I will ask the Father, and he will give you another Helper, who will stay with you forever. He is the Spirit, who reveals the truth about God. The world cannot receive him, because it cannot see him or know him. But you know him, because he remains with you and is in you.

"When I go, you will not be left all alone; I will come back to you. In a little while the world will see me no more, but you will see me; and because I live, you also will live. When that day comes, you will know that I am in my Father and that you are in me, just as I am in you.

"Those who accept my commandments and obey them are the ones who love me. My Father will love those who love me; I too will love them and reveal myself to them."

Judas (not Judas Iscariot) said, "Lord, how can it be that you will reveal yourself to us and not to the world?"

Jesus answered him, "Those who love me will obey my teaching. My Father will love them, and my Father and I will come to them and live with them. Those who do not love me do not obey my teaching. And the teaching you have heard is not mine, but comes from the Father, who sent me.

"I have told you this while I am still with you. The Helper, the Holy Spirit, whom the Father will send in my name, will teach you everything and make you remember all that I have told you."

John 14.15-26

God's Spirit leads me into all truth

Jesus said:

"I did not tell you these things at the beginning, for I was with you. But now I am going to him who sent me, yet none of you asks me where I am going. And now that I have told you, your hearts are full of sadness. But I am telling you the truth: it is better for you that I go away, because if I do not go, the Helper will not come to you. But if I do go away, then I will send him to you. And when he comes, he will prove to the people of the world that they are wrong about sin and about what is right and about God's judgment. They are wrong about sin, because they do not believe in me; they are wrong about what is right, because I am going to the Father and you will not see me any more; and they are wrong about judgment, because the ruler of this world has already been judged.

"I have much more to tell you, but now it would be too much for you to bear. When, however, the Spirit comes, who reveals the truth about God, he will lead you into all the truth. He will not speak on his own authority, but he will speak of what he hears and will tell you of things to come. He will give me glory, because he will take what I say and tell it to you. All that my Father has is mine; that is why I said that the Spirit will take what I give him and tell it to you."

John 16.4b-15